Blinera Nikqi was born in Kosovo, Peje. She came as a refugee in 1995, at the age of 3, to Germany, accompanied by her mother and brother. She grew up in Stuttgart, where she also went to school. Elementary as well as high school. She is fluent in Albanian, English, and German. Beginning at age 21, she travelled to New York twice, where she stayed for a couple of months. She is very self-aware and regards herself as having a "Diamond Mind."

I dedicate the book to all the people whom I have been hurt by: My True Love, God and My Soul. Nikolai

Blinera Nikqi

ENIGMAS FRAGMENTS

AUSTIN MACAULEY PUBLISHERS™

LONDON • CAMBRIDGE • NEW YORK • SHARJAH

A CIP catalogue record for this title is available from the British Library.

ISBN 9781035864614 (Paperback)
ISBN 9781035864621 (ePub e-book)

www.austinmacauley.com

First Published 2024
Austin Macauley Publishers Ltd®
1 Canada Square
Canary Wharf
London
E145AA

Moving

Moving in and out is something I doubt
'Cause through the time, I stayed online
For a new home to call mine,
I need a shelter to shine,
And be able to climb
To new highs
And forget all the lies.
I was misused so many times,
To be able to forgive,
I tend to shift
Away and above, my own dove,
I look like a hove,
That still sits and fits
Everywhere she goes,
I call myself a delve!

Why?

Why do I still live,
for the sake of forgiveness,
I tend to give less,
of what I care,
I don't want to share,
my own being,
but later sacrifice,
my feeling
I wish for death,
'cause life is nothing but enduring,
so, I keep better furying,
about now and then,
never underestimate my glam!

What To Do, But to Hope

Don't know what to do, but to hope
full of misused, but nope
I won't permit to quit,
'cause I came to do shit,
nothing I want to lit,
is all I care about & forbid,
the unlocked & rid,
of all the noises & stay fit,
but above all, I want to hit,
the last time of my Life,
is all I care about, w/o a knife,
stay by my side like a might,
a mighty heart,
shines through like a fart,
that sets the world free,
is all I want to agree.

I Would Like to Write

I would like to write a book,
rewrite my Look,
stand up to my feet & shook,
all about me,
is she,
who agree,
to deep,
I keep,
myself like a sheep,
guarded & held,
by God's lead,
I will never bleed!

I Was at Home

It was first a pleasure,
then it turned into a measure,
I have messed up the day,
but still my slay, was away,
will gain it back,
as soon as I move into vain,
kind of fame,
I tend to over tune the shame,
I once felt so hard,
moved away by a pair of cards,
self-struggled,
no need to feel obstacles,
because by the very end of this summer,
a hummer,
will be my slumber!

Failed

Failed to succeed,
I want to bleed,
until I grow into a seed,
why is it that I still believe,
I aren't nothing without a needle,
in a sand,
I would like to band,
a new me,
is what I need,
please feed,
the Lost sheet,
I can't live,
that's why I'd like to give,
away my Life,
so that I can knife,
me into death,
that's All I wreath,
and feel like I'm on a shelf.

Support

If you don't have support, when you need it,
you don't want it, when it's like a creed
Because, when you needed it badly,
that's when it felt gladly
But when you can give it to yourself,
and then receive it from somebody else,
it's like gras, that can only grow by watered
so, when a flower has to flourish by herself
the flourishment, already took place
Everything besides, without the help
Will always stay, for the process of growment
Like an actual detriment
Because, by having the power of growing on your own
The norm will always stay like a superpower form of a
uniform
By achieving that, you may reach out even other's dorm
Only, don't lose yourself for others
Because they didn't do it for you,
but still call you brothers

Happiness

Happiness is to a place,
it's a just like sweet-bitter taste
Once you felt it,
it overcomes you like a racket
In closed guards, can it be hidden
You tend to break even the forbidden
Close to God's Love & Light,
it shines through sometimes like a fight
A fight for the unreached,
it makes you want to bleed
The blood you taste,
it's like a Chase
But before it's empty and hollow
In you,
you pass by it like a glue
Because you knew back then,
how it's felt to mend

Loving The Light

The light we reach,
might be just like a preach
Preach and reach
But never leach somebody
Because once you tend to teach,
you are like doctrine above
That I which nobody should approach
Reach out for the Light,
and let sometimes somebody decide,
Still knowing for you that you are always Right
Not in their eyes,
but for their mindset price
The price you to pay,
for your honesty and their play

Beautiful Sunday Morning

As I aroused to my feet,
I felt a sudden sun-ray
It shined through my window,
which never seemed struck so hidden
Beautifully slept, dreamed about my love, locked away
We were hugging, and expressing love
Though it felt, undoubted
Really wishing for him to feel the same way,
which is unconditional love and sun-rays
Hoping for the beautiful dreams, to turn reality
So, everything else, is nothing but mandatory
I love you, for you, because that's the deal,
to stay love for,
everything unhealed

Death Related Struggle

First there was endless felt sorrow,
later on, realising, as why I had to borrow
Realising the victim, I was turned on into
Was really made me had a role played on to
Could not, only hope for God's help
But made myself live in a cave
By others formed, only me could harmed
As sad it may sound,
I am telling the truth
So, everybody, can heal in a mentally,
still stable youth

Me Wishing to Be, Not as Pretty as I Am

When you are too beautiful,
sometimes it's a detriment,
Beginning for yourself, because the real power is then hiding,
you not them
The often, self-denying and not self-satisfied woman,
around you, who give you the feeling of being,
envy about you
It makes me feel sometimes, of having to hide and not having
the chance to radiate,
without a devilish stride
I would wish and hope that every single one gets to show,
their inner beauty, combined with hope
because at the end, it's what makes us bold!

A Jealous Demon, Hiding

A jealous demon, hides and wishes bad vibes
But the worst is, when it's in form of a "helping" hand,
in real it's nothing but trying to break the band
Between you and God, the almighty force and Fulfilment inner power,
of heart beating complete happiness,
Just in case, you forget it, keep reminding yourself,
so, it's never breakless,
but always endless!
Endless, just like the unconditional Love and foreseeing Light,
might everything else, always seem bright
Keep your belief, and trust in God, in every situation and moment,
to be able to have a blast!

Wishing Nothing but Release,
In Death Form, Please!

Today I had my last conglomerate, but what I have
Experienced once was again was moral deform,
Am I living for the sake of others,
or being treated every day new like a hatred hovel
Please GOD! Take my soul and welcome me,
With humans on Earth, I don't want to be
Testes and hurt, until I don't care any longer about my
Existence, is something I came across sadly, twisted
But why its hat justice on earth,
has really nothing until it's done
O son, I am just one of them and also none
Forgive me for how I may occur,
just please allow me to cure,
First your heart, so it can ease, and then your soul is for sure
Free and grown, into something delightfully,
parallel to that, kindly and big enough
to catch, but only God can match
and can reach itself a soul which stays undead and by God
always in conglomerate

Hope Encountering

First the mind was manifested,
then the struggle evaluated to a more damaged street menace
I couldn't do what I thought was right,
more like how I felt and then decide
Be it aggressive, loud or chilled
Nothing ever had a smell of chills
Only of grandiose kills
Kills of others boughs bus right
And my own personal delight
A bad-conscious hid me very hard,
then later on
I want to apologise, and try not to think about,
them in congregate
The boughs weren't too bad-modded,
still in the End, they were kind of rooted
I think too much, before I write,
that's when the lines start not to shine

Federal Assembly of Disturbance

This house in Zwiefalten, in all in all
A big haul
Many nationalities, withdrawn
May it be criminals or just humans, with no amount
Of a willing self-crown
Meanwhile, I like to see them,
the criminals, who almost build the walls
There are like my family, because they speak to me and treat
me nicely,
without being tantalising
I really would like to spend some more time with them,
so, I would meet their real reason,
behind their,
now "peasant" living season
Please, allow me to be your friend, also in off-seasons,
so we can together have a moving, almost,
pleasant compare-reason…

Putting Together Words

The way, I rhyme
Must be something I can't deny
The combining words, they don't come from my head
But merely assign
For me it's the most expensive thing, I can rely
Because it fulfils me also, when I am old cannot move
Forward, in my younger tempo line
Happy for me and others that I finally am on my own way of
mind,
and don't decline,
my work-ethic and my talent,
fulfilling me and others too,
so, I will stay unforgotten until,
the rest is pure!

Couple Of Days Off

I haven't wrote for a couple of days,
and it feels as though, I want to drag myself to my knees
Because writing makes me, have a purpose
Without it, I feel as though I've lost my purpose.
Living a life, which make you happy & not others
Is something I require, for all my loving brother's
Let's all celebrate, who we are
Instead of complaining, as why we crawl
Loving yourself first doesn't mean, narcissism
which means that by loving yourself,
you feel love for other too by paralysm
Freedom in your mind first, makes you feel free
But something else really does agree
And that is being honest to all around you,
because at the end,
it will always shine through!

Praying Every Night

I am praying every night,
the last few fights
it doesn't see, to shine like light,
but I am sure it's not never now too tight
for a better rewrite,
of my own special delight
I keep on going as though I feel the night
Not dark, but mighty,
in its own wonderland, height
As dangerous as often, it might seem,
I never show afraid, for other's to keep in a screen,
but want to make my own, work ethic
beam!

Why Does Its Occur to Me

As though I am just one of them in fee
may it be
That I forgot as why to live for free,
I want to break the sphere,
but bounce back every time in anger through mere anxiety,
of freedom that I feel I don't deserve in form of self-controlling monarchy,
I am sorry if I caused any trouble or bad hatred atmosphere,
Really which to receive, what I try to give, which is pure
Love, peace and good chemistry
Please forgive me for every pain in others through me, it
Was not my intention to break a galaxy, which seemed
Not meant for me
What is meant, and what you make yourself count
Should be in one's hand, never rebound
I wish I would not feel haunted.

The Days Passed By

As I quietly sit and cry,
by the Inside
I mourn Life,
as I take the damage by my side
I want to apologise,
for my own sake conscious self-demise
Don't need to blame anybody else for my self-deny,
at the End it's just him & I
Why is it that I had to enter hell alive,
Be it because of my good-by,
That my Loved one's couldn't agree for me to fly,
they'd rather see me in a cage without no breath and die.

Anxiety & Drama

One good aspect anxiety & dramas has,
is that it doesn't last,
pretty sure it comes to an end,
someday or moment prior to e send,
away and in despair,
it has no repair, because my soul is faint away
and I want to have my Life taken to someway,
in God's moving mountains day.

Psychiatrie Zwiefalten

I am wearing pyjamas,
she screamed at me through the door of the maid's room
which has no charm,
I cannot endure one more single drama,
me never wanting to cause bad karma,
I lost it all, by losing me
Please let me regain some self-esteem &
It feels like blasphemy,
which it is,
that's why I have no respect towards me

Psychiatry Tübingen

A shelter I looked for,
later transformed itself into a big hole
Doctors, destroying me
To the point of self-demolition monarchy
Why me,
why not them
Be it an underlying gem,
and more,
like a corridor full of
unattached wardrobe
How heated the hell might be
And the struggle not having an end to foresee
I wish for them lifetime peace & more
Never wanting to mistreat them in doze
Just for the sake of God's justice
I might apologise to them rightly

Missing To Be Missed

As the days come to an end,
I dream of a loyal, caring friend
I really thought, I had nothing to lose more
Finally realising, it was me who, acting on encore
Gladly, I reminded myself, of some of my greatest wishes
Which is indeed, to be a mother, who does not only the dishes
But also, wishes her children to feel free, live happy and not relentless
Caring for themselves first, is what I would hope,
they inherit first,
never cruelness, also much love on first
Most importantly, me wishing for them, they can flourish
So, until they find themselves, they have courage
To speak out and stand for themselves,
In a world full of shatterness, and learn, what it means
To evolve and feel they have an opinion, which counts
So, everything will never seem too loud to sound!

Thursday 28th

This day felt, unlived
even the liveliest receiving gift
did not have something that could shift
the loosing hours and days, pass by
today, even my hand is heavy and it does not supply
what I require from myself, multiply
A day as heavy as it goes by,
I am joyfully, welcome the next days
Forwardly looking, what live can afford, after a stop by
Needing to remind myself, as why I carry on
Which is, my happy lifetime and hopeful mind
Though sometimes shadowed by dusty crowd's
It never has a long-lasting amount, of my wishing
Life's bound,
which is crowned!

Misused

Until using somebody for the sake of others
You really need, to think as why one can borrow
The human mind, upset and not completely taken
As such, it should always, be enough to be able to touch
Much more than being fully able to fought,
is what I would wish, for everybody to be able to bought
But by believing also in the upcoming sought
Finally, regaining the stable human mind, is what should
Be enough to grind
Make sure to carry on, through every sphere in your Life,
until carrying on will be torn,
and the only thing remaining, is like newborn

Do It 4 Yourself!

Don't ever care what others did to you,
Because at the end, starting from the beginning
It was meant to come, the way it came
Always start, with a new self from the Re-gaining
Be sure that whoever did you bad, will get it back
Intensely and will be reminded just like somebody who took crack
Backwardly loses himself,
that's why staying on the safe side and always bright
should be your priority to yourself and keep your smile
To a higher degree of Karma finding, it's Guilt
Never mind why it had had to happen firstly,
but be convinced that it's not lastly,
In a class society, a minimising category of a person
Will higher seeming people always feel like winning
Be careful, a position can have a last word
But the true power is conquering you with the power of Lord!

Climbing

To be able to keep climbing, through desert and long streets
with only rocks
Is a power only God is able to give to a human,
with no visible clocks,
on his arms,
only an amount of charms,
decide whether to wear them visibly or beneath,
by not revealing them, they stay with you
but when you put it out, it's almost sure
to be taken away,
It may take you a long time for yourself to get it back
Though not for eternal Lost,
Solely grabbed away and tried to be broke
The Rock, God is, will always be there to hold
And always should be told, to your every
Descendant in the world

Optimism Can Build You!

Be optimistic, so your purpose will be
For the sake of yourself is true
Hidden talent and power, until it's for you
Don't try to convince others
Because they will never reach out what you can do,
Stick to your own belief, when it comes to unfolding
Always maintain,
Sustain,
Don't drag, put pain
Aside and rewrite
Yourself almighty
You have a superpower, take it
And make it,
unbreakable, for you
Powerful is power,
when it comes from the heart,
and is available

Scare

When they want to scare you,
don't let it care you,
in the end, it's only like a bear for you,
don't ever allow to share you,
make it responsible and rare you,
so, you find a peaceful not let anybody break you,
admit that you are strong
so, everything besides that is wrong.

Why I Had to Sell My Soul

Getting put in a psychiatry by your mother's testimony,
first,
I couldn't think of something worse,
Never had the intention of feeling like a curse
But once you're out, it's observed
Cannot do something else but reverse,
the bad for the good,
and vice versa,
one day I can feel the atmosphere,
changed and rearranged,
for me, and my own soul first,
Because the struggle is almost brutal,
every day and worse,
why is it that everything is nothing but a wishing purse,
that we, everybody, wishes to get filled
with unconditional love and no remorse,
believe in the miracle,
It can happen and will,
stay marvellous and never kill!

Rape

I was raped,
let alone the mere fact,
that it seems gone,
it follows me like a thick throne,
that I feel, every time more & more,
wishing to overcome my heart core,
that once was like a shore,
cannot withstand my own adore,
by others often almost raped, to this day,
how I seem to shade away,
is almost a miracle,
or God's secured crickale,
I feel his safety,
so sure,
that even, if not seeming pure,
I always manage to feel the cure.

Feeling The Need to Talk

I have the sudden urge of need to talk,
about what happened to me, in any way of walk
don't know what's worse, death and giving up,
or the urge of keep moving until it's like a pop-up,
to have the power of lock-up,
yourself from the world & you, still what's in the head,
it's more of mad,
memories and traumas,
to this day it seems not to have a paradigm,
I feel the need of free me,
to not be in a cage,
till the end of time,
but still a crime,
is what I witness everybody more & more,
the core is like a whore,
no matter as soft, it gets broken,
by envy & hate
so, it makes you want to shade,
away and above,
pray for God's move,
in the name of the pure,
and feel secure!

Beyond My Own Path

Paths you set along yourself, have a power of becoming a true self
Lead the way, as much as you can conquer the way,
that's a rapid slay
Become more of an artist, than a chart list
A uniquely remaining self, beyond yours that's been telled
Underlie your points, without begging for coins
Know who you are, by being a star
Lead yourself in a morally world yours,
you make sure are no toys,
just boys and man with undisputed faints
I know who I am, that's why I can
I can become anybody, but never insulting or robbing from somebody.

Surprises'

42

Best made, so far, a grade,
steady fade,
but never a saint's
Because by approaching and reaching out,
you will always feel like a big stout,
be grateful, throughout.
Because by that it will all come out,
the worse and manque,
always like a chique,
surrounded and more,
I tend to seem to whore,
even though,
it's just a dough,
I make and break,
by that always like a cake,
bewitch yourself,
so, the spook
will forever feel like a cray.

So Much Time

Has passed away, since I wrote like I was paid,
now feeling the glad, I often so rely on my maid,
I often wonder, how "real" prisoners must feel about their
gone well-fare
Needing time ahead, to misinterpret the diamond kid,
I wish nothing more than Nikolai as my fit
Because to me he is a bit,
like an ungrown misfit,
resembling me to stay truly so like a grit,
that has nothing to lose but her misprint.

Fore-Seeing

The truth is hard to swallow,
may it be to borrow,
anything in the world you can be
just remember to foresee
And dare to be, the true me
Beside a magnificent thee
You are you and that's something deep
Nothing in the world is like a sheep
Innocent and brave,
is all around you like a grave.

When They Give You Evil Eye

It's up to you to decide whether to hide,

still when you feel like there's nothing to decide,

but the point is uptight,

to circulate like a bright,

power of your own might,

always so right,

keep your own slight,

Because at the end who wishes others bad luck and disease,

will be rewarded,

by God with a tease,

even death can occur,

but you need to find a way to cure,

may it be with the help of others or your own strength,

there can always be at the end,

a miracle trend,

uphold and behold,

that God's justice upon who does bad,

one day at a time,

he will everything seem fine,

just keep a dime,

that strengthens you, through every climb and grind!

When You Break Morals

When you break morals,
it comes back to you tenfold,
stay true and make room for new,
better for you, so you can do what's best for who?
But you!
Trust me, to break and mistreat others
Is worse for you than harass your own sorrow,
I recommend you to not command you or others,
Because at the end it will demand your own circumstance,
vanish everything that makes you feel bad and
substitute it with glad,
you can feel and deserve,
only when your moral is a great perform and
matches the norm!

Clown

47

Me in space of grace,
but still got the power to erase,
all the bad around me,
by not feeling fear,
showing mere,
gear,
to spread sheer,
form of love and hormone,
I'd like to encounter everybody fearless,
so, I have to clown,
to build an unseen wall,
that protects me from fall,
Nobody is ever going to break that way,
so, I'd like to maintain that play,
until one day I can show my real slay,
and feel fearless even in despair!

Define Hell

A monstrous way of heat,
I cannot believe,
as to why this is all on my feet,
will there ever be a sheer,
that covers the fire that's in me
how can I manage to manage the thee',
Oh God please rearrange me,
I don't know as to why this is not just flee,
Cannot think of something more miraculously,
than the mere fact that it's just silly,
to think I will ever soon find a dilly,
a dilly place to withstand,
this hell without a helping hand,
somebody that can overcome my circumstance
and think of a better way to let me feel the chance,
to enhance,
and fall in trance,
which seems like a fence,
that protects me in all chance,
and let me glance!

Forgive

For the sake of your conscious,

everything around is nothing but bunches

Try and later cry

Because a Good-bye, will always be in the sky

Become and let welcome

Yourself, by new and few

So, you will have a rule

For you,

to undo,

the crew!

Be Cautious

Everything around, might already
In its form steady,
away and above,
to a limit of a dove,
never too far, but also never too close to shove

Stress

Use it, make it for yourselves mighty case
Block the limits away,
like a well-fair,
never use a good-morning hair,
as a glue sticking in Mair,
compare,
everybody and everything around you,
until there's only care!

Boringness

Either it motivates you,
or brings you to mere despair
Either it makes you get out,
or it lets you have a last rocket mout!

Care

53

Be careful to care more for the ungrateful,
Because at the end it's what makes them greater and full
Feel your power, to overcome what's ever holding
You back and doesn't let you on the track
Freedom in mind first,
afterwards in speech
body and soul,
for you to keep away the demons inside you,
there's always a different side of you!

Attractive (ness)

It occurs, may vanish
May occur and disappear
Let alone, feel your bone
Stone will always be like a prone
Don't stick onto it,
attract will have features that feel like racket
don't allow to maintain only on surface,
because even a beautiful face can be a menace!

Stamped Sick

55

A stamp is a mark,
it has no hidden dark
Put it aside for you,
walking in pride,
so have a room full of tride,
Make your mind and slide!

Where To Hide

Where to hide is the question,
I only might seem too tight myself up,
but please allow me also to show up,
in places where there is also blow up,
and not only slow,
I so much hope for a new rope,
where I can cover in like a dope seeming
steam, but in real it's only a deem,
where I tend to feel like a cream,
covering up and facing others,
which otherwise would be not allowable,
as for me in form of showering!

Abundance

57

Reliance,
back-lance,
even fiancé,
has a re-sphere,
I might occur,
on the abundance,
is everything but mandate
to me to feel radiant to thee'

Poesie

All that is in me,
through registered gee,
I want to be,
the real me,
so let me flee,
and sooner or later gear,
around like a sheer,
good atmosphere.

Evil Eye

Receiving, perceiving
Trustworthy it's never truthy,
but be reassured,
everything comes back,
so, keep your track.
Why it had to happen
It had to happen for me,
so, I can move further in loving memory,
always keep me renomy,
renome,
for me,
to you,
be true,
and never undo
Because it will sew you.

Disturbance

Self-disturbance leading of disturbance others,
makes you feel sorrow,
but only feeling for yourself,
it's what I call a shelve,
where you hide and slide,
away and above,
until everything is under control.

When You Believe

61

Everything can seem mandatory,
be aware that even a secondary can be a
a first dary,
go encourage yourself to boss up,
so, you can floss up,
keep everything straight and don't push so much up,
dare but never care!

Thinking Of Not
Being Able to Write

Is worse than not being able to write itself,
convince your brain and it will always maintain,
the same per habitat,
nothing can drag it down just by bla bla,
always on the safe harbours' bazar,
am I meaning the magazine or the testra,
won't and can't never give up,
because the real test its o be on top,
and still not cop the slop!

Luck

Given, taken
betrayed, delayed
worshipped, man shipped
Brutal, Ritual
By Love, never too late to hold
Be told, never too late to be bold
Stand, make a Grand
New you, for you
always seek out,
for the untold

Powerful

64

For you
through you,
admits you,
in between you,
all along for you,
Conquer!

Love

65

Be mature, to know
that Love is now
It may vanish,
what lasts is the
question,
as to why you loved,
and not powdered,
but shadowed…

Dream

Dream and stream,
the meaner,
should be yours,
for the sake of everybody's condolences,
never try to menace,
solely trace,
the race,
which should be without a case,
living freely in a world full of God's sake.

Anxiety

67

Felt, it's upheld
want to overcome,
can't be done,
just praying with tie,
it will find a dime,
turn it into Lime,
and feel the anxious knot
harmlessly kind,
but mind.

Feeling Of Failure

Feeling, just like everything
is built inside your mind,
try to grind,
after every defeat,
there comes a second leaf,
is the tree built and formed,
by life's norm deformed,
Deformation can exist,
but to last is something
I decided!
so, make up your mind,
and keep the struggle
brave enough for everybody else,
especially you and delve!

Destiny & Faith

You may seem to have a written destiny,
though make it yours,
with prayers and belief,
you can achieve,
anything in the world,
only have a moral last word,
so it carries you on,
by at least a standard norm,
anything can be done,
but be convinced!

Hungry

When you are so hungry,
you feel like you want to fly,
away and up in the air,
so, your hunger has a repair,
for the thirst above,
nothing can make it shove,
like a prof.,
you feel like a catastrophe,
sensing and approving,
I might also have proven,
Myself to better days ahead,
feel the rhyme and you feel the dead.

Greed

Greed of need,
Is something out of reach,
because once you put it out,
it's like a cowed,
and you can never have any,
amount of a new lay-out!

Church

My church became for me a thirst,
for the peaceful surrender,
that even a bartender,
could not be more of a mentor,
for the mind sati zing,
I hope for a more compromising,
surrounding,
so, everything else will be astounding,
but me, once in a while,
I don't want to shine,
But mend my diamond mind.

Where Were You,
When I Fell Apart

The struggle I go through, without knowing about you.

My Life became hell, still I want to be in a shell.

I need somebody to take good care of me, so I can move further in Loving memory.

The hustler I became was part of my shame.

Nothing I endured can make me better off from my self's faithless destiny.

I wish for Love, peace and a grounded fundament, in a world full of regiment.

This world we live in must be an overcoming thing that we once later,

rethink.

Thankful for every breath I can take, may it be in hell or break.

Love has to rule, otherwise we are full of betrayal and cruel.